The Key Facts™ on India

Essential Information on India
By Patrick W. Nee

The Internationalist®
www.internationalist.com

The Internationalist®

International Business, Investment, and Travel

Published by:

The Internationalist Publishing Company

96 Walter Street/ Suite 200

Boston, MA 02131, USA

Tel: 617-354-7722

www.internationalist.com

PN@internationalist.com

Table Of Contents

Chapter 1: Background

The Indus Valley civilization, one of the world's oldest, flourished during the 3rd and 2nd millennia B.C. and extended into northwestern India. Aryan tribes from the northwest infiltrated onto the Indian subcontinent about 1500 B.C.; their merger with the earlier Dravidian inhabitants created the classical Indian culture. The Maurya Empire of the 4th and 3rd centuries B.C. - which reached its zenith under ASHOKA - united much of South Asia. The Golden Age ushered in by the Gupta dynasty (4th to 6th centuries A.D.) saw a flowering of Indian science, art, and culture. Islam spread across the subcontinent over a period of 700 years. In the 10th and 11th centuries, Turks and Afghans invaded India and established the Delhi Sultanate. In the early 16th century, the Emperor BABUR established the Mughal Dynasty which ruled India for more than three centuries. European explorers began establishing footholds in India during the 16th century. By the 19th century, Great Britain had become the dominant political power on the subcontinent. The British Indian Army played a vital role in both World Wars. Years of nonviolent resistance to British rule, led by Mohandas GANDHI and Jawaharlal NEHRU, eventually resulted in Indian independence, which was granted in 1947. Large-scale communal violence took place before and after the subcontinent partition into two separate states - India and Pakistan. The neighboring nations have fought three wars since independence, the last of which was in 1971 and resulted in East Pakistan becoming the separate nation of Bangladesh. India's nuclear weapons tests in 1998 emboldened Pakistan to conduct its own tests that same year. In November 2008, terrorists originating from Pakistan conducted a series of coordinated attacks in Mumbai, India's financial capital. Despite pressing problems such as significant overpopulation, environmental degradation, extensive poverty, and widespread corruption, economic growth following the launch of economic reforms in 1991 and a massive youthful population are driving India's emergence as a regional and global power.

Chapter 2: Geography

Location:
Southern Asia, bordering the Arabian Sea and the Bay of Bengal, between Burma and Pakistan

Geographic coordinates:
20 00 N, 77 00 E

Map references:
Asia

Area:
total: 3,287,263 sq km
country comparison to the world: 7
land: 2,973,193 sq km
water: 314,070 sq km

Area - comparative:
slightly more than one-third the size of the US

Land boundaries:
total: 14,103 km
border countries: Bangladesh 4,053 km, Bhutan 605 km, Burma 1,463 km, China 3,380 km, Nepal 1,690 km, Pakistan 2,912 km

Coastline:
7,000 km

Maritime claims:
territorial sea: 12 nm
contiguous zone: 24 nm
exclusive economic zone: 200 nm
continental shelf: 200 nm or to the edge of the continental margin

Climate:
varies from tropical monsoon in south to temperate in north

Terrain:
upland plain (Deccan Plateau) in south, flat to rolling plain along the Ganges, deserts in west, Himalayas in north

Elevation extremes:
lowest point: Indian Ocean 0 m
highest point: Kanchenjunga 8,598 m

Natural resources:

coal (fourth-largest reserves in the world), iron ore, manganese, mica, bauxite, rare earth elements, titanium ore, chromite, natural gas, diamonds, petroleum, limestone, arable land

Land use:

arable land: 48.83%

permanent crops: 2.8%

other: 48.37% (2005)

Irrigated land:

622,860 sq km (2003)

Total renewable water resources:

1,907.8 cu km (1999)

Freshwater withdrawal (domestic/industrial/agricultural):

total: 645.84 cu km/yr (8%/5%/86%)

per capita: 585 cu m/yr (2000)

Natural hazards:

droughts; flash floods, as well as widespread and destructive flooding from monsoonal rains; severe thunderstorms; earthquakes volcanism: Barren Island (elev. 354 m) in the Andaman Sea has been active in recent years

Environment - current issues:

deforestation; soil erosion; overgrazing; desertification; air pollution from industrial effluents and vehicle emissions; water pollution from raw sewage and runoff of agricultural pesticides; tap water is not potable throughout the country; huge and growing population is overstraining natural resources

Environment - international agreements:

party to: Antarctic-Environmental Protocol, Antarctic-Marine Living Resources, Antarctic Treaty, Biodiversity, Climate Change, Climate Change-Kyoto Protocol, Desertification, Endangered Species, Environmental Modification, Hazardous Wastes, Law of the Sea, Ozone Layer Protection, Ship Pollution, Tropical Timber 83, Tropical Timber 94, Wetlands, Whaling

signed, but not ratified: none of the selected agreements

Geography - note:

dominates South Asian subcontinent; near important Indian Ocean trade routes; Kanchenjunga, third tallest mountain in the world, lies on the border with Nepal

Chapter 3: People and Society

Nationality:

noun: Indian(s)

adjective: Indian

Ethnic groups:

Indo-Aryan 72%, Dravidian 25%, Mongoloid and other 3% (2000)

Languages:

Hindi 41%, Bengali 8.1%, Telugu 7.2%, Marathi 7%, Tamil 5.9%, Urdu 5%, Gujarati 4.5%, Kannada 3.7%, Malayalam 3.2%, Oriya 3.2%, Punjabi 2.8%, Assamese 1.3%, Maithili 1.2%, other 5.9% note: English enjoys the status of subsidiary official language but is the most important language for national, political, and commercial communication; Hindi is the most widely spoken language and primary tongue of 41% of the people; there are 14 other official languages: Bengali, Telugu, Marathi, Tamil, Urdu, Gujarati, Malayalam, Kannada, Oriya, Punjabi, Assamese, Kashmiri, Sindhi, and Sanskrit; Hindustani is a popular variant of Hindi/Urdu spoken widely throughout northern India but is not an official language (2001 census)

Religions:

Hindu 80.5%, Muslim 13.4%, Christian 2.3%, Sikh 1.9%, other 1.8%, unspecified 0.1% (2001 census)

Population:

1,205,073,612 (July 2012 est.)

country comparison to the world: 2

Age structure:

0-14 years: 29.3% (male 187,386,162/female 165,345,284)

15-24 years: 18.2% (male 116,019,042/female 103,660,359)

25-54 years: 40.2% (male 249,017,538/female 235,042,251)

55-64 years: 6.8% (male 41,035,270/female 40,449,880)

65 years and over: 5.6% (male 31,892,823/female 35,225,003) (2012 est.)

Median age:

total: 26.5 years

male: 25.9 years

female: 27.2 years (2012 est.)

Population growth rate:

1.312% (2012 est.)

country comparison to the world: 89

Birth rate:

20.6 births/1,000 population (2012 est.)

country comparison to the world: 86

Death rate:

7.43 deaths/1,000 population (July 2012 est.)

country comparison to the world: 116

Net migration rate:

-0.05 migrant(s)/1,000 population (2012 est.)

country comparison to the world: 117

Urbanization:

urban population: 30% of total population (2010)

rate of urbanization: 2.4% annual rate of change (2010-15 est.)

Major cities - population:

NEW DELHI (capital) 21.72 million; Mumbai 19.695 million; Kolkata 15.294 million; Chennai 7.416 million; Bangalore 7.079 million (2009)

Sex ratio:

at birth: 1.12 male(s)/female

under 15 years: 1.13 male(s)/female

15-64 years: 1.07 male(s)/female

65 years and over: 0.9 male(s)/female

total population: 1.08 male(s)/female (2011 est.)

Maternal mortality rate:

200 deaths/100,000 live births (2010)

country comparison to the world: 54

Infant mortality rate:

total: 46.07 deaths/1,000 live births

country comparison to the world: 49

male: 44.71 deaths/1,000 live births

female: 47.59 deaths/1,000 live births (2012 est.)

Life expectancy at birth:

total population: 67.14 years

country comparison to the world: 161

male: 66.08 years

female: 68.33 years (2012 est.)

Total fertility rate:

2.58 children born/woman (2012 est.)

country comparison to the world: 81

Health expenditures:

2.4% of GDP (2009)

country comparison to the world: 185

Physicians density:

0.599 physicians/1,000 population (2005)

Hospital bed density:

0.9 beds/1,000 population (2005)

Sanitation facility access:

improved:

urban: 54% of population

rural: 21% of population

total: 31% of population

unimproved:

urban: 46% of population

rural: 79% of population

total: 69% of population

HIV/AIDS - adult prevalence rate:

0.3% (2009 est.)

country comparison to the world: 84

HIV/AIDS - people living with HIV/AIDS:

2.4 million (2009 est.)

country comparison to the world: 3

HIV/AIDS - deaths:

170,000 (2009 est.)

country comparison to the world: 3

Major infectious diseases:

degree of risk: high

food or waterborne diseases: bacterial diarrhea, hepatitis A and E, and typhoid fever

vectorborne diseases: chikungunya, dengue fever, Japanese encephalitis, and malaria

animal contact disease: rabies

water contact disease: leptospirosis

note: highly pathogenic H5N1 avian influenza has been identified in this country; it poses a negligible risk with extremely rare cases possible among US citizens who have close contact with birds (2009)

Children under the age of 5 years underweight:

43.5% (2006)

country comparison to the world: 1

Education expenditures:

3.1% of GDP (2006)

country comparison to the world: 129

Literacy:

definition: age 15 and over can read and write

total population: 61%

male: 73.4%

female: 47.8% (2001 census)

School life expectancy (primary to tertiary education):

total: 10 years

male: 11 years

female: 10 years (2007)

Unemployment, youth ages 15-24:

total: 10.5%

country comparison to the world: 100

male: 10.4%

female: 10.8% (2004)

Chapter 4: Government and Key Leaders

Country name:

conventional long form: Republic of India

conventional short form: India

local long form: Republic of India/Bharatiya Ganarajya

local short form: India/Bharat

Government type:

federal republic

Capital:

name: New Delhi

geographic coordinates: 28 36 N, 77 12 E

time difference: UTC+5.5 (10.5 hours ahead of Washington, DC during Standard Time)

Administrative divisions:

28 states and 7 union territories*; Andaman and Nicobar Islands*, Andhra Pradesh, Arunachal Pradesh, Assam, Bihar, Chandigarh*, Chhattisgarh, Dadra and Nagar Haveli*, Daman and Diu*, Delhi*, Goa, Gujarat, Haryana, Himachal Pradesh, Jammu and Kashmir, Jharkhand, Karnataka, Kerala, Lakshadweep*, Madhya Pradesh, Maharashtra, Manipur, Meghalaya, Mizoram, Nagaland, Odisha, Puducherry*, Punjab, Rajasthan, Sikkim, Tamil Nadu, Tripura, Uttar Pradesh, Uttarakhand, West Bengal

note: although its status is that of a union territory, the official name of Delhi is National Capital Territory of Delhi

Independence:

15 August 1947 (from the UK)

National holiday:

Republic Day, 26 January (1950)

Constitution:

26 January 1950; amended many times

Legal system:

common law system based on the English model; separate personal law codes apply to Muslims, Christians, and Hindus; judicial review of legislative acts

International law organization participation:

accepts compulsory ICJ jurisdiction with reservations; non-party state to the ICCt

Suffrage:

18 years of age; universal

Executive branch:

chief of state: President Pranab MUKHERJEE (since 22 July 2012); Vice President Mohammad Hamid ANSARI (since 11 August 2007)

head of government: Prime Minister Manmohan SINGH (since 22 May 2004)

cabinet: Union Council of Ministers appointed by the president on the recommendation of the prime minister

elections: president elected by an electoral college consisting of elected members of both houses of Parliament and the legislatures of the states for a five-year term (no term limits); election last held in July 2012 (next to be held in July 2017); vice president elected by both houses of Parliament for a five-year term; election last held in August 2007 (next to be held in August 2012); prime minister chosen by parliamentary members of the majority party following legislative elections; election last held April - May 2009 (next to be held no later than May 2014)

election results: Pranab MUKHERJEE elected president; percent of vote - Pranab MUKHERJEE 69.31%, Purno SANGMA - 30.69%

Legislative branch:

bicameral Parliament or Sansad consists of the Council of States or Rajya Sabha (a body consisting of 245 seats up to 12 of which are appointed by the president, the remainder chosen in staggered elections by the elected members of the state and territorial assemblies; members serve six-year terms) and the People's Assembly or Lok Sabha (545 seats; 543 members elected by popular vote, 2 appointed by the president; members serve five-year terms)

elections: People's Assembly - last held in five phases on 16, 22-23, 30 April and 7, 13 May 2009 (next must be held by May 2014)

election results: People's Assembly - percent of vote by party - NA; seats by party (as of 15 May 2009) - INC 206, BJP 116, SP

23, BSP 21, JD(U) 20, AITC 19, DMK 18, CPI(M) 16, BJD 14, SS 11, AIADMK 9, NCP 9, TDP 6, RLD 5, CPI 4, RJD 4, SAD 4, independent 9, other 29, vacant 2; note - seats by party (as of February 2013) - INC 204, BJP 115, SP 22, BSP 21, JD(U) 20, AITC 19, DMK 18, CPI(M) 16, BJD 14, SS 11, AIADMK 9, NCP 9, TDP 6, RLD 5, CPI 4, RJD 4, SAD 4, independents 9, other 31, nominated (INC) 2, vacant 2

Judicial branch:

Supreme Court (one chief justice and 25 associate justices are appointed by the president and remain in office until they reach the age of 65 or are removed for "proved misbehavior")

Political parties and leaders:

Aam Aadmi Party or AAP [Arvind KEJRIWAL]; All India Anna Dravida Munnetra Kazhagam or AIADMK [J. JAYALALITHAA]; All India Trinamool Congress or TMC [Mamata BANERJEE]; Bahujan Samaj Party or BSP [MAYAWATI]; Bharatiya Janata Party or BJP [Rajnath SINGH]; Biju Janata Dal or BJD [Naveen PATNAIK]; Communist Party of India or CPI [A.B. BARDHAN]; Communist Party of India-Marxist or CPI-M [Prakash KARAT]; Dravida Munnetra Kazhagam or DMK [M.KARUNANIDHI]; Indian National Congress or INC [Sonia GANDHI]; Janata Dal (United) or JD(U) [Sharad YADAV]; Nationalist Congress Party or NCP [Sharad PAWAR]; Rashtriya Janata Dal or RJD [Lalu Prasad YADAV]; Rashtriya Lok Dal or RLD [Ajit SINGH]; Samajwadi Party or SP [Mulayam Singh YADAV]; Shiromani Akali Dal or SAD [Parkash Singh BADAL]; Shiv Sena or SS [Uddhav THACKERAY]; Telugu Desam Party or TDP [Chandrababu NAIDU]; note - India has dozens of national and regional political parties; only parties with four or more seats in the People's Assembly are listed

Political pressure groups and leaders:

All Parties Hurriyat Conference in the Kashmir Valley (separatist group); Bajrang Dal (religious organization); India Against Corruption [Anna HAZAREI]; Jamiat Ulema-e Hind (religious organization); Rashtriya Swayamsevak Sangh [Mohan BHAGWAT] (religious organization); Vishwa Hindu Parishad [Ashok SINGHAL] (religious organization) other: numerous religious or militant/chauvinistic organizations; various separatist groups seeking greater communal and/or regional autonomy; hundreds of social reform, anti-corruption, and environmental groups at state and local level

International organization participation:

ABEDA, ADB, AfDB (nonregional member), ARF, ASEAN (dialogue partner), BIMSTEC, BIS, BRICS, C, CD, CERN (observer), CICA, CP, EAS, FAO, FATF, G-15, G-20, G-24, G-77, IAEA, IBRD, ICAO, ICC (national committees), ICRM, IDA, IFAD, IFC, IFRCS, IHO, ILO, IMF, IMO, IMSO, Interpol, IOC, IOM, IPU, ISO, ITSO, ITU, ITUC (NGOs), LAS (observer), MIGA, MONUSCO, NAM, OAS (observer), OECD, OPCW, PCA, PIF (partner), SAARC, SACEP, SCO (observer), UN, UNCTAD, UNDOF, UNESCO, UNHCR, UNIDO, UNIFIL, UNISFA, UNITAR, UNMISS, UNOCI, UNSC (temporary), UNWTO, UPU, WCO, WFTU (NGOs), WHO, WIPO, WMO, WTO

Diplomatic representation in the US:

chief of mission: Ambassador Nirupama RAO

chancery: 2107 Massachusetts Avenue NW, Washington, DC 20008; note - Consular Wing located at 2536 Massachusetts Avenue NW, Washington, DC 20008

telephone: [1] (202) 939-7000

FAX: [1] (202) 265-4351

consulate(s) general: Atlanta,Chicago, Houston, New York, San Francisco

Diplomatic representation from the US:

chief of mission: Ambassador Nancy J. POWELL

embassy: Shantipath, Chanakyapuri, New Delhi 110021

mailing address: use embassy street address

telephone: [91] (011) 2419-8000

FAX: [91] (11) 2419-0017

consulate(s) general: Chennai (Madras), Hyderabad; Kolkata (Calcutta), Mumbai (Bombay)

Key Leaders:

Pres.	**Pranab MUKHERJEE**

Vice Pres.	**Mohammad Hamid ANSARI**
Prime Min.	**Manmohan SINGH**
National Security Adviser	**Shivshankar MENON**
Dep. Chmn., Planning Commission	**Montek Singh AHLUWALIA**
Min. of Agriculture	**Sharad PAWAR**
Min. of Chemicals & Fertilizers	**M. K. ALAGIRI**
Min. of Civil Aviation	**Ajit SINGH**
Min. of Coal	**Shriprakash JAISWAL**
Min. of Commerce & Industry	**Anand SHARMA**
Min. of Communications & Information Technology	**Kapil SIBAL**
Min. of Culture	**Chandresh Kumari KATOCH**
Min. of Defense	**A. K. ANTONY**
Min. of Earth Sciences	**Jaipal Sudini REDDY**
Min. of External Affairs	**Salman KHURSHID**
Min. of Finance	**Palaniappan CHIDAMBARAM**
Min. of Food Processing Industries	**Sharad PAWAR**
Min. of Health & Family Welfare	**Ghulam Nabi AZAD**
Min. of Heavy Industries & Public Enterprises	**Praful PATEL**
Min. of Home Affairs	**Sushil Kumar SHINDE**
Min. of Housing & Urban Poverty Alleviation	**Ajay MAKEN**
Min. of Human Resource Development	**Mallipudi Mangapati Pallam RAJU**
Min. of Labor & Employment	**Mallikarjun KHARGE**
Min. of Law & Justice	**Ashwani KUMAR**
Min. of Mines	**Dinsha J. PATEL**
Min. of Minority Affairs	**K. Rahman KHAN**
Min. of New & Renewable Energy	**Farooq ABDULLAH**
Min. of Overseas Indian Affairs	**Vayalar RAVI**
Min. of Panchayati Raj	**V. Kishore Chandra DEO**
Min. of Parliamentary Affairs	**Kamal NATH**

Min. of Personnel, Public Grievances, & Pensions	**Manmohan SINGH**
Min. of Petroleum & Natural Gas	**M. Veerappa MOILY**
Min. of Planning	**Manmohan SINGH**
Min. of Railways	**Pawan Kumar BANSAL**
Min. of Road Transport & Highways	**C. P. JOSHI**
Min. of Rural Development	**Jairam RAMESH**
Min. of Science & Technology	**Jaipal Sudini REDDY**
Min. of Shipping	**Govind Karuppiah VASAN**
Min. of Social Justice & Empowerment	**Kumari SELJA**
Min. of Steel	**Beni Prasad VERMA**
Min. of Textiles	**Anand SHARMA**
Min. of Tribal Affairs	**V. Kishore Chandra DEO**
Min. of Urban Development	**Kamal NATH**
Min. of Water Resources	**Harish RAWAT**
Min. of State (Independent Charge) for Consumer Affairs, Food, & Public Distribution	**K. V. THOMAS**
Min. of State (Independent Charge) for Corporate Affairs	**Sachin PILOT**
Min. of State (Independent Charge) for Development of North-Eastern Region	**Paban Singh GHATOWAR**
Min. of State (Independent Charge) for Drinking Water & Sanitation	**Bharatsinh Madhavsinh SOLANKI**
Min. of State (Independent Charge) for Environment & Forests	**Jayanthi NATARAJAN**
Min. of State (Independent Charge) for Information & Broadcasting	**Manish TEWARI**
Min. of State (Independent Charge) for Micro-, Small, & Medium Enterprises	**K. H. MUNIYAPPA**
Min. of State (Independent Charge) for Power	**Jyotiraditya Madhavrao SCINDIA**
Min. of State (Independent Charge) for	**Srikant JENA**

Statistics & Program Implementation	
Min. of State (Independent Charge) for Tourism	**K. CHIRANJEEVI**
Min. of State (Independent Charge) for Women & Child Development	**Krishna TIRATH**
Min. of State (Independent Charge) for Youth Affairs & Sports	**Jitendra SINGH**
Head, Dept. of Atomic Energy	**Manmohan SINGH**
Head, Dept. of Space	**Manmohan SINGH**
Governor, Reserve Bank of India	**Duvvuri SUBBARAO**
Ambassador to the US	**Nirupama RAO**
Permanent Representative to the UN, New York	**Hardeep Singh PURI**

Flag description:

three equal horizontal bands of saffron (subdued orange) (top), white, and green, with a blue chakra (24-spoked wheel) centered in the white band; saffron represents courage, sacrifice, and the spirit of renunciation; white signifies purity and truth; green stands for faith and fertility; the blue chakra symbolizes the wheel of life in movement and death in stagnation

note: similar to the flag of Niger, which has a small orange disk centered in the white band

National symbol(s):

the Lion Capital of Ashoka, which depicts four Asiatic lions standing back to back mounted on a circular abacus, is the official emblem; the Bengal tiger is the national animal

National anthem:

name: "Jana-Gana-Mana" (Thou Art the Ruler of the Minds of All People)

lyrics/music: Rabindranath TAGORE

note: adopted 1950; Rabindranath TAGORE, a Nobel laureate, also wrote Bangladesh's national anthem

Chapter 5: Economy

Overview:

India is developing into an open-market economy, yet traces of its past autarkic policies remain. Economic liberalization, including industrial deregulation, privatization of state-owned enterprises, and reduced controls on foreign trade and investment, began in the early 1990s and has served to accelerate the country's growth, which has averaged more than 7% per year since 1997. India's diverse economy encompasses traditional village farming, modern agriculture, handicrafts, a wide range of modern industries, and a multitude of services. Slightly more than half of the work force is in agriculture, but services are the major source of economic growth, accounting for nearly two-thirds of India's output, with less than one-third of its labor force. India has capitalized on its large educated English-speaking population to become a major exporter of information technology services and software workers. In 2010, the Indian economy rebounded robustly from the global financial crisis - in large part because of strong domestic demand - and growth exceeded 8% year-on-year in real terms. However, India's economic growth began slowing in 2011 because of a tight monetary policy, intended to address persistent inflation, and a decline in investment, caused by investor pessimism about domestic economic reforms and about the global situation. High international crude prices have exacerbated the government's fuel subsidy expenditures, contributing to a higher fiscal deficit and a worsening current account deficit. In late 2012, the Indian Government announced reforms and deficit reduction measures to reverse India's slowdown. The outlook India's medium-term growth is positive due to a young population and corresponding low dependency ratio, healthy savings and investment rates, and increasing integration into the global economy. India has many long-term challenges that it has not yet fully addressed, including poverty, inadequate physical and social infrastructure, limited non-agricultural employment opportunities, inadequate availability of quality basic and higher education, and accommodating rural-to-urban migration.

GDP (purchasing power parity):
>$4.735 trillion (2012 est.)
>
>country comparison to the world: 4
>$4.492 trillion (2011 est.)
>$4.205 trillion (2010 est.)
>note: data are in 2012 US dollars

GDP (official exchange rate):
>$1.947 trillion (2012 est.)

GDP - real growth rate:
>5.4% (2012 est.)
>
>country comparison to the world: 50
>6.8% (2011 est.)
>10.1% (2010 est.)

GDP - per capita (PPP):
>$3,900 (2012 est.)
>
>country comparison to the world: 164
>$3,700 (2011 est.)
>$3,500 (2010 est.)
>note: data are in 2012 US dollars

GDP - composition by sector:
>agriculture: 17%
>industry: 18%
>services: 65% (2011 est.)

Labor force:
>498.4 million (2012 est.)
>
>country comparison to the world: 2

Labor force - by occupation:
>agriculture: 53%
>industry: 19%
>services: 28% (2011 est.)

Unemployment rate:
>9.9% (2012 est.)
>
>country comparison to the world: 108
>9.8% (2011 est.)

Population below poverty line:

29.8% (2010 est.)

Household income or consumption by percentage share:

lowest 10%: 3.6%

highest 10%: 31.1% (2005)

Distribution of family income - Gini index:

36.8 (2004)

country comparison to the world: 76

37.8 (1997)

Investment (gross fixed):

30% of GDP (2012 est.)

country comparison to the world: 19

Budget:

revenues: $171.5 billion

expenditures: $281 billion (2012 est.)

Taxes and other revenues:

8.8% of GDP (2012 est.)

country comparison to the world: 209

Budget surplus (+) or deficit (-):

-5.6% of GDP (2012 est.)

country comparison to the world: 166

Public debt:

51.9% of GDP (2012 est.)

country comparison to the world: 60

50.5% of GDP (2011 est.)

note: data cover central government debt, and exclude debt
instruments issued (or owned) by government entities other than
the treasury; the data include treasury debt held by foreign entities;
the data exclude debt issued by subnational entities, as well as
intra-governmental debt; intra-governmental debt consists of
treasury borrowings from surpluses in the social funds, such as for
retirement, medical care, and unemployment; debt instruments for
the social funds are not sold at public auctions

Inflation rate (consumer prices):

9.2% (2012 est.)

country comparison to the world: 195

8.9% (2011 est.)

Central bank discount rate:

5.5% (31 December 2010 est.)

country comparison to the world: 62

6% (31 December 2009 est.)

note: the Indian central bank's policy rate - the repurchase rate - was 8% during December 2012

Commercial bank prime lending rate:

10.8% (31 December 2012 est.)

country comparison to the world: 90

10.19% (31 December 2011 est.)

Stock of narrow money:

$342.3 billion (31 December 2012 est.)

country comparison to the world: 16

$305.7 billion (31 December 2011 est.)

Stock of broad money:

$1.451 trillion (31 December 2012 est.)

country comparison to the world: 15

$1.293 trillion (31 December 2011 est.)

Stock of domestic credit:

$1.402 trillion (31 December 2012 est.)

country comparison to the world: 14

$1.249 trillion (31 December 2011 est.)

Market value of publicly traded shares:

$1.015 trillion (31 December 2011)

country comparison to the world: 9

$1.616 trillion (31 December 2010)

$1.179 trillion (31 December 2009)

Agriculture - products:

rice, wheat, oilseed, cotton, jute, tea, sugarcane, lentils, onions, potatoes; dairy products, sheep, goats, poultry; fish

Industries:

textiles, chemicals, food processing, steel, transportation equipment, cement, mining, petroleum, machinery, software, pharmaceuticals

Industrial production growth rate:

4.8% (2011 est.)

country comparison to the world: 68

Current account balance:

-$80.15 billion (2012 est.)

country comparison to the world: 192

-$46.91 billion (2011 est.)

Exports:

$309.1 billion (2012 est.)

country comparison to the world: 18

$305 billion (2011 est.)

Exports - commodities:

petroleum products, precious stones, machinery, iron and steel, chemicals, vehicles, apparel

Exports - partners:

UAE 12.7%, US 10.8%, China 6.2%, Singapore 5.3%, Hong Kong 4.1% (2011)

Imports:

$500.3 billion (2012 est.)

country comparison to the world: 9

$490 billion (2011 est.)

Imports - commodities:

crude oil, precious stones, machinery, fertilizer, iron and steel, chemicals

Imports - partners:

China 11.9%, UAE 7.7%, Switzerland 6.8%, Saudi Arabia 6.1%, US 4.9% (2011)

Reserves of foreign exchange and gold:

$287.2 billion (31 December 2012 est.)

country comparison to the world: 10

$297.9 billion (31 December 2011 est.)

Debt - external:

$299.2 billion (31 December 2012 est.)

country comparison to the world: 30

$287.5 billion (31 December 2011 est.)

Stock of direct foreign investment - at home:

$256.6 billion (31 December 2012 est.)

country comparison to the world: 21

$232.7 billion (31 December 2011 est.)

Stock of direct foreign investment - abroad:

$121.3 billion (31 December 2012 est.)

country comparison to the world: 28
$106.3 billion (31 December 2011 est.)

Exchange rates:

Indian rupees (INR) per US dollar -
53.17 (2012 est.)
46.671 (2011 est.)
45.726 (2010 est.)
48.405 (2009)
43.319 (2008)

Fiscal year:

1 April - 31 March

Chapter 6: Energy

Electricity - production:
    880 billion kWh (2010 est.)
    country comparison to the world: 7
Electricity - consumption:
    637.6 billion kWh (2009 est.)
    country comparison to the world: 7
Electricity - exports:
    519 million kWh (2009 est.)
    country comparison to the world: 62
Electricity - imports:
    10.53 billion kWh (2009 est.)
    country comparison to the world: 23
Electricity - installed generating capacity:
    189.3 million kW (2009 est.)
    country comparison to the world: 6
Electricity - from fossil fuels:
    69.9% of total installed capacity (2009 est.)
    country comparison to the world: 108
Electricity - from nuclear fuels:
    2.2% of total installed capacity (2009 est.)
    country comparison to the world: 29
Electricity - from hydroelectric plants:
    20.9% of total installed capacity (2009 est.)
    country comparison to the world: 91
Electricity - from other renewable sources:
    7% of total installed capacity (2009 est.)
    country comparison to the world: 28
Crude oil - production:
    897,300 bbl/day (2011 est.)
    country comparison to the world: 24
Crude oil - exports:
    0 bbl/day (2009 est.)
    country comparison to the world: 130
Crude oil - imports:

2.768 million bbl/day (2009 est.)

country comparison to the world: 5

Crude oil - proved reserves:

8.935 billion bbl (1 January 2012 est.)

country comparison to the world: 20

Refined petroleum products - production:

3.226 million bbl/day (2008 est.)

country comparison to the world: 7

Refined petroleum products - consumption:

3.292 million bbl/day (2011 est.)

country comparison to the world: 6

Refined petroleum products - exports:

812,100 bbl/day (2008 est.)

country comparison to the world: 9

Refined petroleum products - imports:

380,900 bbl/day (2008 est.)

country comparison to the world: 16

Natural gas - production:

46.1 billion cu m (2011 est.)

country comparison to the world: 21

Natural gas - consumption:

61.1 billion cu m (2011 est.)

country comparison to the world: 13

Natural gas - exports:

0 cu m (2011 est.)

country comparison to the world: 88

Natural gas - imports:

12.15 billion cu m (2011 est.)

country comparison to the world: 24

Natural gas - proved reserves:

1.154 trillion cu m (1 January 2012 est.)

country comparison to the world: 25

Carbon dioxide emissions from consumption of energy:

1.696 billion Mt (2010 est.)

country comparison to the world: 4

Chapter 7: Communications

Telephones - main lines in use:

    32.685 million (2011)

    <u>country comparison to the world</u>: 10

Telephones - mobile cellular:

    893.862 million (2011)

    <u>country comparison to the world</u>: 2

Telephone system:

    <u>general assessment</u>: supported by recent deregulation and liberalization of telecommunications laws and policies, India has emerged as one of the fastest growing telecom markets in the world; total telephone subscribership base exceeded 900 million in 2011, an overall teledensity of roughly 75%, and subscribership is currently growing more than 20 million per month; urban teledensity now exceeds 100% and rural teledensity is steadily growing

    <u>domestic</u>: mobile cellular service introduced in 1994 and organized nationwide into four metropolitan areas and 19 telecom circles each with multiple private service providers and one or more state-owned service providers; in recent years significant trunk capacity added in the form of fiber-optic cable and one of the world's largest domestic satellite systems, the Indian National Satellite system (INSAT), with 6 satellites supporting 33,000 very small aperture terminals (VSAT)

    <u>international</u>: country code - 91; a number of major international submarine cable systems, including Sea-Me-We-3 with landing sites at Cochin and Mumbai (Bombay), Sea-Me-We-4 with a landing site at Chennai, Fiber-Optic Link Around the Globe (FLAG) with a landing site at Mumbai (Bombay), South Africa - Far East (SAFE) with a landing site at Cochin, the i2i cable network linking to Singapore with landing sites at Mumbai (Bombay) and Chennai (Madras), and Tata Indicom linking Singapore and Chennai (Madras), provide a significant increase in the bandwidth available for both voice and data traffic; satellite earth stations - 8 Intelsat (Indian Ocean) and 1 Inmarsat (Indian

Ocean region); 9 gateway exchanges operating from Mumbai (Bombay), New Delhi, Kolkata (Calcutta), Chennai (Madras), Jalandhar, Kanpur, Gandhinagar, Hyderabad, and Ernakulam

Broadcast media:

Doordarshan, India's public TV network, operates about 20 national, regional, and local services; a large and increasing number of privately-owned TV stations are distributed by cable and satellite service providers; by 2011, more than 100 million homes had access to cable and satellite TV offering more than 700 TV channels; government controls AM radio with All India Radio operating domestic and external networks; news broadcasts via radio are limited to the All India Radio Network; since 2000, privately-owned FM stations have been permitted and their numbers have increased rapidly (2007)

Internet country code:

.in

Internet hosts:

6.746 million (2012)

country comparison to the world: 17

Internet users:

61.338 million (2009)

country comparison to the world: 6

Chapter 8: Transportation

Airports:
>352 (2012)
>country comparison to the world: 22

Airports - with paved runways:
>total: 251
>over 3,047 m: 21
>2,438 to 3,047 m: 59
>1,524 to 2,437 m: 74
>914 to 1,523 m: 83
>under 914 m: 14 (2012)

Airports - with unpaved runways:
>total: 101
>over 3,047 m: 1
>2,438 to 3,047 m: 4
>1,524 to 2,437 m: 6
>914 to 1,523 m: 42
>under 914 m: 48 (2012)

Heliports:
>41 (2012)

Pipelines:
>condensate/gas 2 km; gas 9,596 km; liquid petroleum gas 2,152 km; oil 7,448 km; refined products 10,486 km (2010)

Railways:
>total: 63,974 km
>country comparison to the world: 4
>broad gauge: 54,257 km 1.676-m gauge (18,927 km electrified)
>narrow gauge: 7,180 km 1.000-m gauge; 2,537 km 0.762-m gauge and 0.610-m gauge (2009)

Roadways:
>total: 3,320,410 km (includes 200 km of expressways) (2009)
>country comparison to the world: 3

Waterways:
>14,500 km (5,200 km on major rivers and 485 km on canals suitable for mechanized vessels) (2012)

country comparison to the world: 9
Merchant marine:
total: 340
country comparison to the world: 29
by type: bulk carrier 104, cargo 78, chemical tanker 22, container 14, liquefied gas 11, passenger 4, passenger/cargo 15, petroleum tanker 92
foreign-owned: 10 (China 1, Hong Kong 2, Jersey 2, Malaysia 1, UAE 4)
registered in other countries: 76 (Cyprus 4, Dominica 2, Liberia 8, Malta 3, Marshall Islands 10, Nigeria 1, Panama 24, Saint Kitts and Nevis 2, Singapore 21, unknown 1) (2010)
Ports and terminals:
Chennai, Jawaharal Nehru Port, Kandla, Kolkata (Calcutta), Mumbai (Bombay), Sikka, Vishakhapatnam
Shipyards and Ship Building:
Shipyards: 13
Ships Built: 33 (2009)

Chapter 9: Military

Military branches:

Army, Navy (includes naval air arm), Air Force, Coast Guard (2011)

Military service age and obligation:

18 years of age for voluntary military service; no conscription; women may join as officers, but for noncombat roles only (2011)

Manpower available for military service:

males age 16-49: 319,129,420

females age 16-49: 296,071,637 (2010 est.)

Manpower fit for military service:

males age 16-49: 249,531,562

females age 16-49: 240,039,958 (2010 est.)

Manpower reaching militarily significant age annually:

male: 12,151,065

female: 10,745,891 (2010 est.)

Military expenditures:

2.5% of GDP (2006)

country comparison to the world: 61

Chapter 10: Transnational Issues

Disputes - international:

> since China and India launched a security and foreign policy dialogue in 2005, consolidated discussions related to the dispute over most of their rugged, militarized boundary, regional nuclear proliferation, Indian claims that China transferred missiles to Pakistan, and other matters continue; Kashmir remains the site of the world's largest and most militarized territorial dispute with portions under the de facto administration of China (Aksai Chin), India (Jammu and Kashmir), and Pakistan (Azad Kashmir and Northern Areas); India and Pakistan resumed bilateral dialogue in February 2011 after a two-year hiatus, have maintained the 2003 cease-fire in Kashmir, and continue to have disputes over water sharing of the Indus River and its tributaries; UN Military Observer Group in India and Pakistan has maintained a small group of peacekeepers since 1949; India does not recognize Pakistan's ceding historic Kashmir lands to China in 1964; to defuse tensions and prepare for discussions on a maritime boundary, India and Pakistan seek technical resolution of the disputed boundary in Sir Creek estuary at the mouth of the Rann of Kutch in the Arabian Sea; Pakistani maps continue to show its Junagadh claim in Indian Gujarat State; Prime Minister Singh's September 2011 visit to Bangladesh resulted in the signing of a Protocol to the 1974 Land Boundary Agreement between India and Bangladesh, which had called for the settlement of longstanding boundary disputes over undemarcated areas and the exchange of territorial enclaves, but which had never been implemented; Bangladesh referred its maritime boundary claims with Burma and India to the International Tribunal on the Law of the Sea; Joint Border Committee with Nepal continues to examine contested boundary sections, including the 400 square kilometer dispute over the source of the Kalapani River; India maintains a strict border regime to keep out Maoist insurgents and control illegal cross-border activities from Nepal

Refugees and internally displaced persons:

refugees (country of origin): 100,003 (Tibet/China); 68,152 (Sri Lanka); 9,161 (Afghanistan); 6,621 (Burma) (2011)

IDPs: at least 506,000 (about half are Kashmiri Pandits from Jammu and Kashmir) (2012)

Illicit drugs:

world's largest producer of licit opium for the pharmaceutical trade, but an undetermined quantity of opium is diverted to illicit international drug markets; transit point for illicit narcotics produced in neighboring countries and throughout Southwest Asia; illicit producer of methaqualone; vulnerable to narcotics money laundering through the hawala system; licit ketamine and precursor production

Other Key Facts™ Titles

All Key Facts™ Titles are Available at

www.Amazon.com

THE
INTERNATIONALIST®.
2013